W0038317

The World Underneath

The World Underneath

Poems by

Richard Tayson

The Kent State University Press

Kent, Ohio

© 2008 by Richard Tayson
ALL RIGHTS RESERVED

Library of Congress Catalog Card Number 2007044983

ISBN 978-0-87338-948-8

Manufactured in the United States of America

The Wick Poetry Series is sponsored by the Stan and Tom Wick Poetry
Center and the Department of English at Kent State University.

Library of Congress Cataloging-in-Publication Data

Tayson, Richard, 1962–
     The world underneath : poems / by Richard Tayson.
          p. cm.
     ISBN 978-0-87338-948-8 (pbk. : alk. paper)∞
     I. Title.
          PS3570.A986W67 2008
          811'.54—dc22   2007044983

British Library Cataloging-in-Publication data are available.

12 11 10 09 08   5 4 3 2 1

*This book is dedicated to all children—
born, unborn, and otherwise.*

CONTENTS

ACKNOWLEDGMENTS

My gratitude to my mother, Kathy, my brother, Bob, and my sister-in-law, Laura.

To Rohan Sooklall (stalwart muse), love.

Thanks to the following people:
Alicia Suskin Ostriker, whose friendship and work have been with me every inch of the way, and Mary Crow, whose comments helped shape this book and whose home kept us comfortable. A great big thanks to Maggie Anderson, for her generosity and keen eye. Thanks to Daisaku Ikeda, role model and intrepid peace activist. To Claudette Coughenour and her many miracles. To Sharon Olds and Galway Kinnell, whose lessons are with me still. To Fiona Wilson, Angela Chapin Huntington, Laura Sherwood Rudish, and Lucia Hamet, for their friendship and advice. My appreciation to the Colorado gang—Theresa Kratzer and Jim Spotts, for lending us their wilderness, Deanna Ludwin, Matthew Cooperman, the Reker family, Carol Schmelzer, and Cynthia Mitchell. To Charles Flowers, Hilda Raz, Ted Genoways, Richard Schneider, Marilyn Hacker, and Joan Larkin, for their support of my work. To Will Underwood, Brett Neff, Mary Young, everyone at the Kent State University Press, and to the Wick family, for making the publication of this book possible.

Acknowledgment is made to the following publications, in which these poems first appeared:
Academy of American Poets Web site ("Arms"), *Bloom* ("I Do"), *Colorado Review* ("New Mother"), *The Gay & Lesbian Review Worldwide* ("Whatever Happens to the Lesbian Happens to Me"), *Nightsun* ("On the Way to See James Dean"), *Prairie Schooner* ("Arrival" and "Crowning"), *Virginia Quarterly Review* ("Dark Theater" and "Return," under the title "First Night"), *Washington Square* ("Home," under the title "Home Birth").

"I Do" was reprinted in the anthologies *I Do / I Don't: Queers on Marriage* (Suspect Thoughts Press, 2005), *Family Matters: Poems on Families* (Bottom Dog Press, 2005), and *Velvet Avalanche* (Sajah Projects, Canada, 2006). "Crowning" also appears in *Family Matters.*

"Arrival" and "Crowning" won *Prairie Schooner's* 2004 Edward Stanley Award for Poetry.

My gratitude to the New York Foundation for the Arts for a 2003 Artist's Fellowship, which aided in the completion of this book.

In memoriam:
Ted Drake
Martha "Babe" Simerson
Julie Courtney
Tory Dent
Amanda Goodwin
Michael Daley
Ann Beckerman
Liza Nelligan

I.

O for God's sake
they are connected
underneath . . .

—"Islands," Muriel Rukeyser

THE WORLD UNDERNEATH

A woman whose laugh I love,
whose body has been carefully
   opened, siphoned, drudged

   up from under the deep sea
knell, who with a hook
   in her left breast and a diving

   mask rose and fell, body
burgeoning to an unwieldy swell,
   who, minus blubber

   and ruby flesh, weighed
two kilos less, waterlogged
   found herself discharged,

   healed—.
You would never know,
   as she faces me, both elbows

   on white linen, that she's
older than my mother, and worried
   about the weather: *79 degrees*

   in November, and the leaves
just starting to fall. . . . We're both
   touched with *melancholia,*

   and I go down the road (leafless)
that leads to the son I never had,
   the one who thinks I escaped

   scot-free with his dad, and now
stares at two computer images
   of Earth, each composite's blues

and greens turning bruised
purple, plum-black at Earth's
   center, two hundred miles

   above, dated nine months
apart, the later one clouded
   by a dark zone, partial

   cataract grown in ratio
to the hole in the heavens
   getting larger.

   The nine-year-old who is not
mine, who may be me
   as a boy or you, if you like

   the idea of space and
black holes, nano-
   seconds and string

   theory, if you believe
in the enterprise of exploding
   stars you read about and how

   an ice sheet the size of Rhode Island
fell into the sea on a Saturday,
   once and once only,

   79 degrees in November. . . .

                              •

On Thursday . . . a locustlike cloud of charged particles
shot out of the Sun at more than two million miles an hour,
swarming Earth just after midnight.
      THE NEW YORK TIMES, NOVEMBER 25, 2003

You were looking up at the sun, remember?
At the ever-shine of it, the bone-white

field of it. When you looked away after
you saw your mother

in her dark glasses, tree-tall, her
hand a branch you swung from in the time

before you knew there was time,
her voice saying, "Don't stare

at the sun, it'll make you
go blind." Her dress bright, the waves

rocking toward you, the sea
refracted, your mother holding

her shoes by the straps in one
hand, the other takes you by the wrist,

—remember?—which is
when you realize this skin is yours

and she will always be
yours in a way the swimmers

and waves, red umbrellas
and the jetty going out,

fried fish from the restaurant on the pier
she takes you to each summer

are not yours, the words
white letters you sound out

for the first time—PETE'S
BEACH GRILL—

are *beyond* you, sand
crystals underneath your feet.

                                                    •

The town where I was born
has been on fire since Saturday.
Not all the houses,
but most. A woman crouches
in a place that looks bombed.
Smoke rises in pillars.
She holds up
a half-burnt piece of paper
and her face shines with what
looks like joy. Face
of *having been found,*
face of *not having lived
in vain.* Voice-over tells us
it's what's left of her diary.
She holds it by the edges,
the way someone would

who has just arrived on earth,
touched down in San Bernardino,
sky the color of ash, ground
composed of ash, some
charred posts where a porch
used to be.

                                           •

   Ten below. I'm walking
over the Canadian glacier
   with my brother.

   T-bar, cliff dives,
black diamond runs,
   smokestack town below.

   We clamp into our skis,
start down the mogal
   slope, when suddenly

   the snow rages into a
meltwater river. We swim
   over pocked craters

   and I start to go under,
see my mother's charred
   nightgown knotted

   at my feet, and my brother's
boys—Jeremy, age five,
   Benny, four—floating

past us, their faces
under water, their eyes
     staring straight at me.

And then the water starts to burn.

                                        •

My brother faces me,
the bay window behind him.

I feel good, I think
I'm laughing at something

I did, some mistake
I've made and am learning

to forgive, leaning
against a doorframe in the hot room.

My brother's eyes
are dark, eyelid skin

pale, thin as flesh covering
old bones. But he's thirty-eight,

and if I'd looked closer,
I would have seen the red tinge,

the swelling. "Mom died in her sleep
last night," he says, simple as that.

Of course I don't believe him!
He's joking; our mother

can't *die!* "And you should think
about crying," he says, "seeing

she gave you birth
and all." I've never seen

my brother cry, never heard him
talk like this. Then

I wake up, my mouth
burning, sun bright in my eyes.

•

You could say we're headed
in the right direction, advanced

technology, sexy
buttons to push, cures

for every disease just around
the corner. Each day

Linda's hair gets longer,
Alicia writes her rage

beside the ineffable beauties,
wants to use Power-

Point to project masterful
paintings on the wall

to complement her poems.
Julie made it into the bone

trial, Kate varies her cocktail
and will likely die by natural

causes, which is not the way
Liza died, not the way

Anne B. died, or the woman
whose beauty stunned me,

the dark color of her skin
when she leaned forward

and with labored breath
wrote it down, then read it

to the rest of us gathered
in the circle. Granted Carly

sings on *Good Morning
America,* has a future

and Janet injects
her remaining breast

with mistletoe—I turn
off the TV, unconvinced.

•

The panic attacks began
the summer my mother's gold watch

was stolen from my apartment
above the expressway. The air

so hot it was hard
to sleep, to breathe, to count

cloned sheep or sing
love songs from the time

before we learned to fear
sun, water, fruit,

and seed. *Just the cars,*
I told myself, exhaust

from SUVs headed
to the Island for long

summer weekends, just the sun
colliding with concrete, reflecting

off the high-rise across the street,
fumes I could see only

when the light flashed down just right.

•

My friend visits my class of twenty-two
expectant faces, says the year 2050.

There is a window in one corner
but it is small. Dark green leaves

in the frame. "Your children's
children," she says, "flesh

of your flesh." They look at her
the way nineteen-year-olds do,

full of boredom, full of hope, the face
of the last person they kissed floats

dreamlike toward them. They look
sleepy and want the world

to go away. Rain
has been falling hard all week.

"Spring rain in November," I hear her say,
looking at Caroline's lovely hair,

at the intelligence in Asma's eyes,
at Tashalee who is always late.

At Stacy who had a panic attack
last week and had to stop the car.

At Natalie who told me she might be
going crazy, doesn't want the baby.

Across the courtyard dogwood
bursts into flame, into flower.

                                        •

   79 degrees in November. . . .
And here's the white
   orchid, my wise friend

ordering wine again,
staring out window glass,
   like floodwater

suspended in midair. *Spring*
will be a little late this year,
   I say—and there

is the laugh like no other,
rising up from where
   three children have come,

scattering like confetti,
snow, stardust, or sun
   motes we can't see

but know are there
even on the grayest
   of days, a stonecast

from where people fell
like stones, heavy
   souls slipped inside a

body once only. We drink
our wine, as a shaft
   of light, gold

as summer, flares
down outside and everyone
   in our grateful world goes quiet.

II.

Should we have stayed at home,
wherever that may be?

—Elizabeth Bishop

ARRIVAL

The first day at my brother's house,
I woke on New York time and climbed
down from the top bunk, careful
not to wake the woman in the front
room, lying on her side, mirror
of the child within her, her belly
rising with the regularity of science.
I spooned coffee, thought how
efficient the body is, its arterial
highways and service roads of veins,
aortic arches, ventricles, and atriums,
sulcus terminalis and inferior vena cava,
everything working to keep the baby
alive, ready to slide down
the last slippery curve and arrive
here, in the Milky Way galaxy, third
planet from the sun. Speck of dust
supporting another speck of universal
dust, I see the phone, that essential
device for speaking with those near
and far, friend or enemy, one
pulsar east or just next door,
it begs me to make the call. I open
the sliding glass door, brush today's
paper aside, and dial the number
slowly, fearing he doesn't miss me,
or he slept in someone else's arms
last night, twenty-seven subway stops
from home—but he answers on first ring,
as if he's been waiting to confirm
I didn't die in a plane wreck
over one of the nineteen states
that still puts people like me
in prison. O Texas, O Tennessee,

sweet Georgia with your one-to-twenty
years felony, I flew over canyons
and fruited plains, my crimes
against nature carefully concealed
in my back pocket, my identity
contained at each turbulent updraft
we came to, I didn't flirt
with flight attendants or speak
my name to strangers, and here
I am, making the first call
to the man I'll one day marry.
He tells me how big the bed is,
with its one nebula instead of two,
how wide the frying pan with its single
pancake star, and I tell him not to worry,
Laura will have the baby any day,
and I'll fly fast as the speed of light home.
He tells me he saw the meteor shower
with his mother and son last night, and it's
as if I'm hearing his voice for the first
time, my consciousness inside the receiver,
listening hard to the sound from his throat
and how his throat is part of the six-foot
body which once passed through the portal
of a very small woman. So I lift
my cup to Sylvie, swallow two
gulps of coffee, whisper a pagan
prayer to my own mother, feeling
newspaper gloss beneath my fingers,
the headline at my feet: *Found:*
2 Planetary Systems—Astronomers
Stunned. I tell him
about dimmed failed stars, and no matter

the distance between the Milky Way
galaxy and the Andromeda galaxy,
no matter what laws Congress
enacts against us or how many
times we're beaten and left to die
on a fence in the middle of nowhere,
this man will always be with me.

INDUCED LABOR

Her due date passes,
the temperature rises

past 90 before eight A.M.,
requiring heroic

strength to shift
six inches to the left,

muscular craft to grab
the arm rest and hoist

her upper body 90 degrees
in vertical space, place

the pillow at the small
of her back where the torque

is tightest, the pressure
most unbearable. Something

must be done,
so she punches out

the numbers, taps
her fingers against the phone

console, tells the midwife
she can't see her feet

or eat anything that won't
give her gas, can't stand it

another minute. She listens
to the voice on the other

end, then throws the receiver
on the floor, moves graceful

as a trapped boar into the kitchen
and yells *She wants me to have*

a castor oil shake. Her face
is flushed red as the fiery

world the baby floats in, back-
paddling toward the dream of being

a breathing human, as I take
the blender and scoop

ice cream, add milk
then pour the whole bottle

of castor oil in, think
how men can never know

what it's like to have a world
inside you. She tells me

in language like code:
cervix dilation, caesarian,

the *epidural* whispered
between clenched teeth.

I lift the blender, pour the un-
godly mixture, and she closes

her eyes, crosses her chest,
spoons the first mouthful

of true grit in, acrid medicine,
touching the cool glass

to her cheek, praising the bitter
taste of what's about to begin.

COLD CLOTH

The woman
about to give birth
stands above and stares

into the water,
the way a sailor
looks at the sea

for signs of weather—
blessing or disaster
at the edge of the known

universe. Leans
her thighs and belly
against the tin tub's rim

then puts a hand in, bending
forward, lifts a leg, touches
one palm to the universe

within, her husband
helping steady her
for the climb and hoist in.

She lies there unmoving,
all of us watching her break
into a sweat, her neck

glistening, the midwife feeling
Laura's face then asking
my mother to get a wet cloth

from the kitchen. Mother's face
shows pleasure at proving
she belongs on Earth, and I

remember, at fifteen,
watching her lift the lid
from potatoes she'd grown

in the garden, digging
her fingers in the dirt, mother
scrubbed the skins, cut off

the dead ends, scraped
and peeled each nightshade fruit,
until sweat shone on her neck.

I always wondered why she kept
the house so clean, each ficas leaf
dusted, everything folded in its place.

It wasn't until I was twenty-eight
that she told me how her father
undid her in the dark, his breath

on her neck, a chill
deep inside her. No
wonder my mother jumps

off the couch and fills
the best bowl in the house
with ice water, carrying it

to the daughter with a high fever.
She presses the cloth to Laura's face,
and I realize she's soothing

her own skin, as three generations meet
she's going back to the girl with buckteeth
whose beauty is split open

night after night—wringing out
the wrinkles as Laura breathes
deep, sinks deeper down.

DENKAR AVENUE, GARDENA,
CALIFORNIA, 1951

Suddenly, my grandfather stopped pulling
his daughter's panties down, he held her

by the waist, placed
a callused and huge

hand over her mouth, his own breath
arrested. Then he heard it

again, the metallic jostle
of keys, easy fit of one

in the lock, and before
he could get her panties up and fix

the pink bow in the center
of my mother's hair, smooth

her dress and set her glass-eyed
there, in the middle of the room,

his wife walked in. The person
who is telling you this doesn't know

what happened next, but there
had to have been the buttoning

of a sleeve, the running to the arms
of a mother who let the keys

fall to the floor then stared
at the man she'd married and the girl

she'd given life to. And what
did he feel, this man who drank too much

and drove 18-wheelers
up the coast, delivering produce,

Earth's bounty, to local markets?
Did self-made flesh feel better

than skin of women he could buy
at every truck stop, L.A. to Frisco?

Did his sorry fingers itch when he lay
down drunk most nights, the bourbon

air cleansing him like prayer?
And that day where

was his son, the one
who would remember,

years later, the snug fit
of a man's hand in the small

of his back, in his hair, the father
who would do anything to forget—drink,

smoke, try to take his life with a razor
in the backseat of a parked car?

But for now, we are trapped in the moment
Martha finds Jay, the stiff sway

of birds of paradise, the rice paper skins
of bougainvillea rubbing the lattice

above the porch. Nine years later,
my mother won't breast feed or know how

to hold children in her arms and kiss
their hurt away, she'll later say

she never felt what it's like to come.
O, she'll be a big eater, we'll all

drink too much, kids growing up
to smoke dope on street corners,

graduating to crosstops and white
powder cut into lines with razors

reflected in dorm room mirrors.
But for now a mother drops her keys,

bends to retrieve them,
yanks her only daughter

by the arm and hauls her
into the bathroom, strips her down

to the bare bone, holds her
up to the mirror so the girl sees

the fear in her face, and is lowered
down to the tub, feels

her head go under, then rise
in hands that scrub her skin and inner

mouth, whittling her body
down to its pink shine.

CROWNING

The midwife says the baby's head
is crowning, I can see it
just beyond the vestibulum,
pink vestibule where the child
awaits the appointed hour,
hesitating before the midwife's
hands. Overripe plum in patches,
the forehead becomes more human
each minute, appearing flat,
at first, then yielding its curves
to the midwife's palms as they
usher the tiny body forward,
past the fornix and flesh curtain
of labia majora. Laura's
face is also dark, swollen
with effort, her body
not quite ready, prone
in the water her husband and I
heated two hours ago, her head
now cradled in my brother's hands.
This, then, is the crowning
of the next generation, the feudal
lord of Sonoma, California
passing on the land and its riches
to the child dropping slowly down—
cranium, glabella, temple—through
creased labia minora, color
of the crocus unfurling. The midwife
leans forward and is the first
to touch this infant skull,
her expression registers awe
at the thought of it,
and it happens quicker now,
Laura arches her back, her belly
rises out of the water, everything

in the house now holy—domed
portal, narthex, nave, niched
saints in Corinthian columns,
all of us postulants in waiting.
Laura makes deep guttural
sounds as the child's head
is released from the other world
into the blood-flecked water
of this earth, and all of us
lean closer, see the mother
and child in mirrored relation,
the maker and the made at the center
of the effort to separate.

HOME

The midwife yelled "Get her out
of the water now," so my brother
heaved his wife over the lip
of the tub, and as he laid her
on the carpet, we could see
the baby's head, eggplant
purple, swollen, and still,
protruding from Laura's vagina.
Everything went quiet, my mother
dried her eyes, Bob
quit trying to open Laura's legs,
the midwife's assistant stopped praying,
and Laura lay still. Then the midwife
broke the silence with a phrase
I'd never heard before, *shoulder
dystocia,* and the world began
to move again, the five of us
crowded closer around the mother,
each one holding a part of her body—
leg, arm, ankle, elbow—
my mother pressed a cool cloth
to Laura's forehead while the midwife
put her hands around the baby's head
and pulled. Laura didn't look
like she was breathing,
and just when I thought she might be
dying, her ribcage
heaved and my brother began
to cry, silently at first, then louder,
his head cradled against his wife's
breasts, and in between
sobs he whispered into Laura's ear.
She opened her eyes and didn't
seem to know her living room or who

her husband was, she didn't remember
that Benny was asleep in his bed,
and Jeremy out for the night—
she began to move again, heaving
hard, and her body
opened, the gleaming lips quivered
then pulled back in their flexible
beauty, and the midwife got part
of her hand into Laura's body. "That's
it! That's it! Push enough
to let the shoulders out, someone
hold her feet, O Jesus, someone
help me get this one's shoulders
out." Laura moaned and started
to shake, which must have scared Bob,
because he lifted his head and yelled,
"Someone call 911 now!"
My mother couldn't find the phone
so she went to look in Raina's room,
Laura moved her head from side
to side, and the midwife tried
to pry the baby like a barnacle
from underneath a rock, when
suddenly Laura opened wider
and the baby's shoulders slipped free.
We all let out an audible sigh,
and the room filled with champagne
bubbles, a spontaneous parade
began down Main Street, the baby
on top of the highest float, the midwife
at the loudspeaker, her voice rising
above the crowd: "Thank you
God, thank you, it's coming
now, easy, easy, push

easy, it's almost
here." Laura closed her eyes,
contracted one last time,
and Gabriel slipped gleaming
into the midwife's hands.

FIRST BREATH

after Linda Gregg

By the time you breathed your first breath
the five of us feared you might be dead,
and your mother lay so still we thought
she might be dead. The midwife lifted you
from your mother, and I tried to forget

that the last child the midwife had taken
from another woman's womb had died
in her hands, no explanation, and now
the midwife listened to your heart,
slipped the suction into your mouth.

The things in the room took on a quality
they'd not had before your mother lay down
on the floor, her hair wet and tangled
as a girl who had almost drowned
before her husband jumped in

and dragged her up the riverbank,
hauled her onto dry land. You lay
like the desecrated body in Giotto's
painting of Jesus, five women touching him.
One has his feet in her palms, which is

how the midwife touched you after
she'd put you on your mother's belly.
Another holds his wrist, as my own mother
had touched your fingers, each one wrinkled
as if in old age, checking to be sure

you were all there. In Giotto's version,
Mary's face is in profile, one arm

beneath her son's head, eyes open, Mary's
grief apparent in the downturn
of her mouth, her lips so close to Jesus,

she will kiss him. And since joy does not
arrive without grief, your father bent
in his weeping toward you, and without
cleansing your face, arched over his wife's
breast and kissed you. In the Giotto,

two women with their backs to us, as if
their grief should not be seen, and if
seen, not described, their heads draped
in muslin, their mantled shoulders slumped.
Which is not exactly the position I took,

but it was close—I knew the shock
of the only girl I'd loved, returning
without our child inside her, twenty-two
years earlier, that sorrow still lives
within me, in the room in which

you almost died. Three of the women
and the body of Jesus have gold halos,
as if knowing the spirit up close.
I had my notebook open and was willing
to write down death in order to keep

something of you alive: if you had died
I wanted to record all of it, to look death
face-to-face, and know it. All the mysteries
have gold halos. The sun was gold at 6:56
in the morning. The angels above ringed

in gold, their wings lending them
the illusion hummingbirds contain,
above the inert body. Then you hurled
the living scream, stone-heavy and weightless
as light, pure passion, at us, the lamentation

became joy. Christians wept and prayed,
non-Christians looked down and wept—
your mother lifted her hand to your face,
and a shaft of light penetrated the room, lungfuls
of song praising the suffering you had just begun.

DARK THEATER

Make no mistake: when you were born,
the world did not want you. Did not

need another with precisely
your dormant talents. Stars

shine of their own accord, not
because of you, as they say

in songs someone will one day play
for you, looking in longing

down at your face as you wish
upon stars in dark theaters,

soundtracks or actresses
singing songs of romance,

the way dreamers do.
And the lover next to you

will touch your hand as if
that could save you.

Make no mistake—
consolation ministers false comfort,

the gods will not keep you safe
from this moment on, clever

words are mostly wrong. And though
yours was a difficult birth, no one

promised otherwise, despite
what the romantics say, the ones who wake

in the wee small hours of the morning
to a familiar face they do not recognize,

receding hairline, body bulges, the aching
lush-life back. The earth

more beautiful than ever. Endangered.
As time goes by you will have a lawn

you desire to trim, to mow, roses
tied to the porch, dug up after divorce.

Regardless of a bolt out of the blue, moonglow,
solid earth temporarily beneath your feet.

RETURN

My first night home, after
we'd kissed a long time
then drunk half a bottle
of wine, tasting summer
orchard heavy with the heat
they say you must pass through
to enter the gates of heaven,
removing your shoes and cotton
socks for the journey, un-
buttoning your shirt, pearl
by glaucous pearl, we lay
down in the king-sized bed.
I listened to your breathing
the sound full of teeth-
whisper and throatcall,
as if fifteen days apart
had made you a stranger to me,
I leaned over and wanted
you inside me. I pressed
my lips to yours, tasting
amber apple tempered
with a tinge of darker hours,
and our bed touched the tip
of the Pearly Gates. O, we
could not stop there, we blew
clouds to the left, celestial
dust to the right, half-
expecting God to show up
in his marriage hearse, we
stripped away the rest
of our earthly belongings—
chinos, Levis, leaf
and vine—we got down
to the silk underwear

of our souls, and before
the locked gates of heaven
we said our vows. No state
lines to stop us, no born-agains
to spit on us, sea to shining sea,
how we fell asleep like that.
But night won't let us get away
with such simple joy—your snoring
woke me, and at the threshold
of sleep I heard an infant's cries
rise up through the floor, as if
in dream, the child whose birth
I'd traveled to witness
had flown 2,572 miles east
in his best stretch booties
to be with us here.
Since I've always wanted
a child, I try to wake you
to remind you there is
a future. You grab
my arm in sleep, as if
to keep what's already yours,
and before I wake fully and know
the sounds growing louder
are hunger cries
from the newborn below,
I remember the pain
of a woman about to shock a soul
from the ethers, place it
inside a body
once only. You
roll away from me, and I
sink down in the warm
indentation you have made.

III.

The will to change begins in the body not in the mind

—ADRIENNE RICH

I DO

I bought the rings at R. J. White Jewelers
from the old man with cataracts
who handed me the black velvet tray,
like a silver tureen reflecting black
orchids at the reception after
we'd kissed. I took
the tray and as I started to shake,
he told me to try one on for size,
then turned his back and blew
dust and dried rose petals
from the mantle. "Been in business
forty years," he said, rubbing
his finger over a smudged
mirror. So I chose the one
with tiny grooves etched
along the edge, I put it on
my ring finger, left hand—what
was I doing, this was not something
I could have planned for
or foretold, once done
it could never be cancelled.
"That's nice," he said, and told me
how he'd opened the shop in 1963,
same location, two hundred thirty dollars
to spare and a love of metals
that alchemized to liquid gold
under fire. "Back then
there weren't too many boys like you
buying rings, no sir. This was
before Stonewall, of course."
It had been years since I was called
a boy, and I thought how I was seven
the day in 1969 those men
in skirts and high heels stood up,
three blocks away, for the lives

of people like me who would one day
walk into a shop and buy a ring
for another man's finger. "You sure
this will fit him," I asked, looking
down at that perfect gold
circle, like a halo that would taste
of fire if I put it on my tongue
and swallowed. He patted my hand,
the way a grandmother would
and said, "If it doesn't, bring him in
and I'll serve the champagne I keep
chilled in back for special occasions."
R. J. winked then, and a white
poodle appeared, as if the dog knew
those syllables of drink by heart,
and I supposed they'd been living there,
together, since 1963, watching the years
go by like the parade passing
down Christopher each fourth
Sunday in June. *Let me not
to the marriage of true minds
admit impediments,* so I gave him
five hundred eighty-six dollars
and held in my hand the velvet case,
soft as my lover's palm, and went
to the Stonewall Bar to pay
my debt of gratitude with two
sips of gin and the feel
of names carved in the countertop:
*Michael loves Robert,
Bill + Guillermo forever.*
I started to get sentimental,
so I took the F train home and found
him on the couch in his underwear,

I held him for a long time, kissed
his lips and the room crowded close
around us, everyone we loved
took a seat, relatives alive
and dead, friends alive
and dead, everyone who had been
imprisoned for kissing in public,
the ones who were tortured
and had their tongues cut out,
the ones kept in boxes
the size of the body, the ones
tied to a fence and beaten
in the name of God. In front
of them all, I held the hand
of the man I loved
and said I wanted him in my life
for as long as I have my life.
His eyes welled up, and I tasted
salt in the corners of my mouth,
then I tasted his salt inside
my mouth as we
married each other
in front of the Van Wyck Expressway
at 6:15 on June 8th, a Tuesday
which will never repeat itself.

ARMS

I'm late for the birth-
day party, it's one
of those cool after-

noons when the world
is clear, is made
of glass, the sky

so blue you want to
look up at the very
center of its pupil

in case you get
a glimpse of what
comes after

we leave here. I'm
thinking my lover's
sister is 32

today, but I want
to let time stand
still, let the tourists

go on waving their
America-the-Beautiful
flags across 49th

Street, let the three
ladies whose hair
is the color of smoke

rising and ghosts
taking leave of their
senses go on laughing,

near the fountain, may
we all not have
a care in the world.

It's August 23rd, I must
get on the train, yet
a tree keeps holding

my attention, its leaves
luscious from the summer
rain, there's a canopy

beneath which the Pakistani
man I talked to last
week sells his salty

sauerkraut, lifting
the lid and letting out
steam each time he

serves it over hot
dogs, and the man
pays him, then turns

toward me, his thick
muscled arm tan
in the sun, the tattoo:

BORN
FOR
WAR. The day

is gone, the people
around me gone, I am
trying to remember

that I'm a pacifist,
trying not to pay
attention to his name-

brand shorts and sun-
glasses that won't
let you see a glint

of eye behind them,
I'm trying not to watch
him eat the hot dog in two

bites and nudge the woman
beside him who pushes
a stroller, his arm around

her waist as he pivots and
sees me staring. Yes he might
leap to the right, grab

my throat punch
me shoot me gut
me clean as a fish

taken from the black glass
of the city's river street, but
the church bells are tolling,

people are saying
their prayers three blocks
away in the hushed

dark. So I take a deep
breath and am no longer
here, I haven't been

born yet, there is no state
of California, no Gold
Rush or steam

engine, electricity hasn't
been invented, people
cross open spaces

on horses, no Middle
Passage, and I watch
the Huns kill the Visigoths

who slice the throats
of every living
Etruscan, a crowning

city is razed, the virgins
raped, one nation
fights for land

to walk on, then is
walked on until
someone carves on a cave

wall, then someone
writes on papyrus,
until we do it all

again, right up to
concentration camps, rivers
flowing with nuclear

waste. 49th Street
floods back, and the man
with the tattoo turns

away, as if he's decided
not to crack my skull
open and drink me

on the 965th day
of the new century.
War goes into the fifth month.

The church bells stop,
the ladies get up and walk
toward Radio City

and while I don't believe
in an eye for an eye, I have
a flash lasting no longer

than it takes for a blast
to render this city
invisible, shadow

of a human arm I tear
from its socket, its left
hand gripping the air.

MIDDLE NIGHT

1.
This father tosses
his covers, rolls
away, mumbles

what sounds
like underwater
language, what he'd said

to me today:
*Your problem is
you don't have kids.*

Unlike the Guyanese
couple below, whose
newborn cries in the night;

unlike Chitra at the end
of the hall, whose son
shows me his painting

of a coral reef
with neon fish
swimming through—

I'll never know
what it's like to watch
my child grow: twenty-five

years this month,
she chose to pull up anchor
and let you go.

2.
Among the things I never said
to her, though I sped the length
of California, crossed state lines

to—what? Persuade her?
Stop her? Tell her how
small I felt, bit of magnetic

matter in space, miracle
DNA replicating to the end
of time, finite world,

desert plateau I drove toward,
dark river highway I crossed,
the way my father had done

before me, his father had done
before him. . . . Speeding
across a burning desert,

late arrival. And the living
body we'd made together—
already dead.

3.
You who will never have
one for the road, who
will never crank up the radio

and smell desert heat, dry
with its taste of Oregon
dust, never see the Snake River

because she set you alone
in the flesh-boat of your body,
pushed you out to open sea. . . .

You who will never watch me
move through lessening dark
to lie beside the father

whose son turns nine in September:
you live here, always
in sleep. The emptiness

I feel tonight, looking down
at darkness, is the emptiness
of the cipher who whispers in me still.

WHATEVER HAPPENS TO THE LESBIAN HAPPENS TO ME

after Muriel Rukeyser

Whatever happens to the lesbian
walking down 7th Avenue
at two A.M., not thinking
of danger, touching
the turquoise earring her mother
gave her, new stubble
of the crew cut, wondering
if she went too far, passing
three college boys, drunk,
in front of Snooky's, hearing
one of them slur something
she can't make out
but knows the gist of,

she's remembering Trina's
face in the light and is
not thinking, as she turns
down Garfield, of the dark
street or the still
trees, a dog barking
down the block and how
she'd always walked with eyes
in the back of her head
and doesn't hear
the approach from behind

and is caught dead
mid-thought as someone
cracks a bottle over her
head while someone slams

the pipe into her knees
and someone swings the bat
that cracks her rib, she's

not thinking of anything
but the pain, as she falls
on the concrete in our
human city, her mother
dreaming of a house
in the country, her father
ordering last call,
her brother getting up
to feed the baby, then going
back to sleep, whatever

happens to this woman
who is me and not
me, as she hears a voice
lunging at her over skies
over oceans at a great
distance, a voice

yelling *Stop
it's a woman,* and that
woman hearing six feet
running like six drums
beating in her head

and she thinks *Where
are my glasses?* and touches
the blood on her hand
to the blood on her face
and prays to a god she quit

believing in some time ago,
and thinks, as she tries
to get up, *We're not
separate ever,* and is

changed forever, in the middle
of the night, eight blocks
from my room, whatever
happens to the lesbian
is happening to you asleep,
is happening to me asleep,
safe in my lover's arms.

ON THE WAY TO SEE JAMES DEAN

I hardly notice the man who gets in
at Parsons Boulevard, one seat over
from the man I swore I'd spend
the rest of my life with, read
the Sunday *Times* with, go
to the movies with to see
if James Dean is still

sexy, drinking our coffee, I say
Hon, check this out, showing him
a picture of the Klan leader convicted
forty years after killing the boy
whose body was found floating
in the Tallahatchie, and the man

must have heard, without turning
his head he spits out his words:
Fuckin' faggots, fuckin'
ho-mo-sexuals. Everyone
in the subway car stops
moving, stares into their cups
or at a printed page, and I
can't tell who he's talking about
until he turns toward me, the way
psychos in movies look straight
into the camera when they say
something that makes your spine
freeze: *Fuckin' fairies*
wanna get married. Wish
I had my piece, I'd use it mother
fuckin' faggots. I look down

at my gold band, look over
at Rohan's gold band, I secretly
give up on God, Gandhi,

see myself get up, take my Uzi
from my back pocket, hand
grenade from my left shoe, my ten
queer fingers morph into switch
blades ready to cut his lips
to pieces, I open my eyes, tell
the love of my life *We should move
to another car.* But Rohan

is someone who will not be taken
down a notch or two, he tells me
he doesn't want to, so I pour
white light into the car, *Hail Mary
full of grace, Nam-Myoho-Renge-Kyo,
Vishnu, Sebulisa,* I see the people
from above, the way they say you notice
every detail in times of crisis,
your life flashes before you, and you note
how the white man and the brown
had not kissed or touched, at the moment
of impact you remember every color
and nuance, you see gold
halos above the human orders seated,
you hover over the dark-skinned mom
who sits stock still, Bible
in her lap, staring at the man as if
daring him to come one inch
closer to her two pink-ribboned girls
clutching her arms in terror, you love
your neighbor, the Chinese woman
with her bag of Chinese cabbage,
the red-haired eighteen-year-old
who presses his chest into the back
of his raven-haired girlfriend, you admire

the tenacity of the Jewish man reading
from his book of prayers, each word silent
on his lips, and you love the black man
with his cane, the two girls in the corner
of the train who might be in love,
the Indian woman in her best sari,
coming home with her husband
from the mandir, which is when

you climb higher, get a wider
view of the world's delicacies, love
the diversity of ocean fish and grains
of sand, love birds of every order,
insects of every hue, the seven
miracle wonders, shore
to shore, continents kissing
other continents, you recognize how
each island, separate to the naked eye,
is connected underneath, and just
as you realize that everybody loves
the planets and the air they swim in,

you come back into the car and have
the chance to love humans of every
persuasion, even the ones who want
to bomb the hell out of every creature
still breathing. *Fuckin'*
wedding rings. I grew up in the hood
and know a faggot when I see one.
He grins at me, the way the female
soldier in the paper smiles
over the pile of naked bodies
she's standing on, ah to be pleasured
by power. There on the brink

I stand, holding pictures of people
whose heads were blown off
during morning prayer in mosques,
four girls whose bodies caught fire
in a southern church, the man
assassinated while he talked
on a porch, people living without
arms, ring fingers buried deep
in the Sunni sand. Jerusalem,
Palestine, Bali, London—on the brink
we stand, until we arrive

at West 4th Street, and we get out of the car,
checking to be sure the man doesn't follow us—
but he stays in his seat, grinning at us
through a window scratched with someone's
initials, he flips us the finger, and the train
disappears, leaving Rohan and me to argue
about the best way to walk to the theater,
we battle it out in front of perfect strangers,
salt on our popcorn, diet or regular soda,
left, right, or center of the screen, and as James
Dean walks toward me, I can't make out
his terribly beautiful words.

SKIN SONG

I hear that sound begin, deep
in his body. And like the one
who lets the body speak,
I press my ear to the hillside
of his pelvis, close my eyes,
and feel his voice rise,
vibrating,
the way one hears a live
catalpa, deep in the forest,
split down its center
and fall. I lie inside
his pelvis, and he extends
the low bough of his arm
to my chest, his face
flushed, his hair shines
like moss on the manzanita,
and I know that inside the trunk
are the rings of his history.
So I count those rings—
and when I get to 40, the song
ascends along his arched back
as I hold his left hand
and kiss gold until his fingers
shake, as if he fears falling
over the sandstone ledge,
the wet skin of song
rises into his mouth, wholly
invisible. Then he
falls on me, and I taste
the dense earth of his mouth,
and in the heave his breath
anticipates the quiet
of my breath, that sound
keeps us from the ordinary world.

TO MARILYN MUSGRAVE,
CONGRESSWOMAN FROM COLORADO

Last night you told Larry King
and the billions

that I want to have sex
with animals, that I am

a polygamist, and this

is just to say
that the man I've married
in the privacy of our house

because my country won't have us
roaming the streets, fucking

every creature in sight
and sometimes trees
and you too if you don't

watch your behind, Congress-
woman—this is just to say

that we're living
on Main Street U.S.A.
where Rohan will turn 41
in November, I'll be 44
in January, we have a cat

named Coltrane and have lived
together five years, sleeping

together, in the same bed
almost every night
(and some afternoons),

and are not married to anyone
but each other. And since

we don't have sex with our cat,
or with any other animals,
or children for that matter,

we've put your words
on our fridge, to have
a laugh while reminding ourselves
what we're up against:

Are you going to have
polygamy day?
Group marriage day?

—our gay fridge
that we'd marry if we could, with all

its gay eggs and, since Rohan
is vegetarian, lots of queer lettuce,

extra-fat cucumbers,
gallon of homo-
genized milk (organic of course).

And don't forget the fruit,
which won't confuse you
we hope.

NEW MOTHER

The day the asteroid large enough to wipe out
Texas hurtles past Earth
at 68,000 miles per hour, I walk
close to the new mother. I stop
near her, read the headline
at the newsstand, see her tighten
the hood of the child
at her chest. She looks

down at the baby's face and is
far from the traffic along
Eighth Avenue, far from
High Holy Days, transported
by the features she's still getting
to know, eyes green
as ocean, hair fine
as kelp beneath the knitted cap,
nose the size of the algae node
floating in the sea, now pink
with cold. The mother

bends closer, and I watch
the globes of her breath warm
her baby's skin, her mouth
almost touching him, as though
she might devour him, blue
booties to spittle
below his chin, baby's
grin, brow, the brain
encased within, trigeminal
nerve, cortex, medulla
oblongata, she looks
down the walk, then at
her baby again. It begins

to snow. The spell
is broken. The mother
looks up at a sky so swollen
it threatens to let loose
the force of nature from within—
she turns and sees me
staring. I am

in awe of how one person could
love, without words or expectation,
another, I look straight
at her, think how the asteroid
called 2001 YB5 is 1,000 feet
in diameter, large enough
to produce the world's worst
disaster if it smashes into
our planet. The mother's

face changes, she senses
danger and eyes me
with suspicion, her expression
convincing me she wouldn't
give it a second thought before
leaping for my throat or casting
her body off the Brooklyn
Bridge, if her child were
floating in the ocean this petite
woman weighing no more than
110 pounds would swim
the length of the Atlantic, anything
to save him. She gauges

the distance between oncoming
cars and doesn't wait

for the *Walk* sign but tucks
her hands beneath her baby's
bottom and dodges a cab, her legs
moving fast, catapulting them
up the curb and on to
the other side. She turns

back and sees me contemplating
extinction, how the asteroid
would unleash 400 times
the death force of the atomic
bomb if human
intelligence cannot blast it
out of the air
in time. She keeps

moving south, and I remember
scientists predicting a mile-long
meteor may strike Earth
in 2027, by which time the baby
will be up for his first promotion,
I'll be sixty-five, and the mother
will be planting her garden
once more in spring.

MY COLONOSCOPY

for Ed

Without anesthetic what I saw
could have been mistaken
for stars, quasar inside
a giant elliptical galaxy, earthrise
over rolling hills of the moon,
deep craters, gamma rays with
a tiny sun off to the left, and above
the domed night sky—I was
shocked at the beauty of my body.
I grabbed the metal rails, held on
and felt as if I were being impaled,
the doctor turned the corner with me,
both of us watching the screen,
the way two boys will stare
at a video game, making
the spaceship dodge asteroids,
exploding stars—and then
the pain stopped. It was as if
I'd risen to a great height
and was now separate
from my body, a god looking
down at one of his children,
knowing that the blue
indentation in Ursa Major
was my liver. The doctor said
we were entering the small
intestine, and the galaxy's
ceiling lowered, we scrunched
down at the shoulders as he
extended a tiny metal jaw
which took three baby bites

of my flesh, the way the long
arm of Apollo had taken three
bags of dust from the moon—
then we were going back fast,
gaining force of gravity,
and down below was planet Earth,
a city, a hospital room on 77th Street
where a man lies on a table
then gets dressed and walks
into the arms of my lover,
who kisses me and we go out
into autumn gold, the universe beyond.

UNDERNEATH THE LEAVES

Dirt

You can't deny it's there
on the TV screen in living color

you're glued to it, the way weather
sticks to our skin in autumn

in winter in summer it's there
and in spring when young lovers hit

the city streets and country roads,
parties in every college town,

it is there—granted they are
men, both twenty-one and living

the college dream, it is dark
and they kiss in front

of the outdoor ATM or is it
outside one of the million beer guzzling

bars that are second homes to both
those who hate themselves and those

who love themselves dearly, is it
Midwest old town square or strip

mall, Northeast Main Street, land
of the brave, the free, the democratically

elected for all, land of pilgrim's pride
where our richly fatted fathers

died, the way this college kid kissing
his boyfriend is about to die, whispering

I love you and laughing in the last
minutes of his life. You watch

the car drive up out of nowhere,
two guys get out, and the skinny

blond is about to be chased, is about to drop
his cell phone during the chase,

is about to crouch low to the ground, quick,
quick—*can you hear me now?*—is about to

be hit over the head with the crow bar held
in the hand of

the man he's never
seen before is

about to shatter
his skull and kick

it until that head is
mashed in like a

watermelon struck
with a sledge-

hammer and split
open. The under-

taker will have to re-
build tissue on his

right cheek, his left
eye.

Even then some fathers will not love
their sons.

Even then some of my people will say
he deserved it.

* * *

At the Natural

Yes countrymen yes
my countrywomen, we have the special

right to watch the eyes of those
who see us kiss hello in the super-

market stare for a second then
roll back in their heads, we have

the special right to see the faces
express disgust, not even thinly

veiled, as we smile and hug
hello, Rohan and I, we are happy

to see each other after he's spent
the day playing basketball or

swimming with his son who turned
nine last month, after I've spent

the day reading up on the many ways
those in my country claim we are

sinful and will go to hell after
we die. Hell

is here, dear friends, we are
living it now, and heaven

resides inside us too, dear
citizens we share this planet with,

eat the bounty of the earth with. You
can reach out your hand to round

melons, touch the glossy green
globes, the tan fleshy pitted

spheres about the size of a baby's
head, which grew in the earth

we walk on together. And we gather
in protest of war or in favor of it,

depending if you believe in the vengeful
version of God who wants to kill the enemy

or not. I confess to setting my sights
on not hating my neighbors, no matter

how challenging some of them make it,
especially when they beat

up break apart stomp dis-
member spit on bury alive or otherwise

desecrate
the body of one of my brothers.

* * *

First Thought on Waking

Seeing the scene in which the hot rod fancy car approaches
two lovers on a dark deserted street, and the big college guys
with aluminum bats get out saying *here faggot come and get*
what you deserve faggot and one of the faggots takes out a gun
calmly aims it and calmly shoots until four drunk college kids
are dead then puts the gun back in his pants doesn't bat an eye-
lash but takes his lover's hand and continues walking.

There are days when I wake up
and actually feel like this.

* * *

Sylvie's House

The first time my lover took me to his mother's house,
she made Guyanese pepper pot
and showed me her altar
of Hindu gods, in the center of which
stood a statue of Jesus, palms open,
facing me.

Rohan baked Christmas cake,
and after we said a prayer

73

for people without
houses or warm coats, kids
whose parents left them
at birth or stuffed them
into dumpsters
somewhere in our famous,
rich cities—we had
a champagne toast.

She's seen the photographs:
her son in Jim's blue kayak,
paddling down the Colorado river;
me in front of the Canadian ski lodge,
tanned and just down from the mountain;
Rohan in his pressed suit on our first date;
the two of us kissing
in front of Karahi Restaurant;
Rohan, his son, and I laughing
in front of last year's Christmas tree.

Over rice kheer she says
she wants me to meet her cousin.
When I ask how she'll introduce me,
she says, "As my son's friend, of course."

* * *

Impromptu

Late fall, the kind of weather
Rohan and I love because we get

out our winter coats to see
if they still fit and take

the train to Cold Spring, New York,
up the Hudson and past the nuclear

reactors. We sprinkle some
glitter, a little gold on top

of those two dark cones, and let
stardust fall and sun-

dust fall into the air and over
the water, over

us all, we let it come down like God-
dust mixed with some mineral

dust from Mars. We try to love
the people who built the reactors

out of stone, out of mortar
and the clay we're made from,

try to love the people
who work there, the ones who need

money to buy broccoli and cat
litter, try to love the governor

who keeps them going, thirty miles
from the millions who live

in their shadow. We sprinkle love-dust
on them in great heaps, like first

snow coming down on this, the one
and only morning like it in the history

of our species, late fall and you're on
the 10:20 Hudson, you're wearing

your heavy coat, the one you love
because it feels warm as another

person hugging you, and you get off
and walk to your favorite French restaurant,

the way we do, exactly
the way we do, holding hands

at the table, and later holding hands
on the streets of Cold Spring, New York.

Difference is, we keep turning
to see who might be

behind us in broad daylight, hell
or high water, who might believe

God wants us dead, laid flat
on a road we don't know the name of,

then run over again. No wonder
with eyes in the back of our heads,

we look at each other and hold that gaze,
saying silly nicknames and laughing,

the way you do when you're in love,
kicking up some red leaves, some gold.